VEGAN
RECIPES
for Newbies

Ana Ortega

Cover design and formatting www.jdsmith-design.com

All enquiries to ana@anaortega.org

First printing, 2013

ISBN 978-1484072028

"Vegetarian food leaves a deep impression on our nature. If the whole world adopts vegetarianism, it can change the destiny of humankind."

Albert Einstein

Newbie in the Vegan world?

Welcome to a new you!

You should be proud of yourself.

Be proud of becoming a newbie in the vegan world because you are learning something new and willing to change. You are pushing yourself to change for the **BETTER**.

You are getting rid of old myths – which is in essence something very hard to do and a big step towards a better **NEW YOU.**

And more importantly you are doing something. You are doing something amazing for yourself.

And just wait because this chapter of your new life from now on can only get better and better.

Whatever the reason for your decision to embrace this new adventure, don't worry, you just got lucky. Here you have your first little vegan bible to help you get started.

Packed not only with lots of vibrant colours but also with vitamins, minerals, proteins and all those essential nutrients you need to rock that body you have!

Whoever said that beautiful healthy food comes expensive at all levels is about to be proven mistaken.

Because becoming vegan has never been this fun.

I challenge you to try each one of these recipes for one week.

I dare you to be very "selfish" just for this one week- to stick to the vegan diet, to silence the little inner voice that tells you that cheese is tasty, that you want that greasy stake. Because there is a reason you got hold of this book. There is a reason why you want to become a better you. And that reason is what makes you who you truly are and that is what matters.

This premium collection of tasty recipes will bring up the creative side of yours in no time. They are easy to make, inexpensive and super healthy for the fresh newbie veggie you are.

I encourage you to try. You will be **REWARDED**. Your reward will be your **HEALTH**. And please do not forget that health is the best reward you will ever get. Isn't that just **SIMPLY AMAZING**?

Lola was a beautiful cook, always busy in the kitchen, relentlessly looking for the perfect recipe while her jealous ugly sisters observed and criticized her.

But Lola did not have time to hear those discouraging comments. Lola had one goal in mind: she had to find the recipe for happiness.

The days passed by and Lola continued trying new ingredients, reviewing the old ones again and again and creating new recipes while meticulously adding them to her notebook.

She started enjoying the feel, smell and taste of spices, the range of colours that unfolded in front of her eyes as if by magic. It is then when she knew she was gifted because she had just found the recipe for happiness.

Be happy in this precise moment. Be happy being who you are.

With Love (because it is all there is),

Ana Ortega

Newbie Veggie Shopping List

Let's begin with your shopping list for this week & the newbie veggie must have cooking tools:

Get that basket full of greens, nuts, spices, fruits, proteins and carbs.

From this moment on you will be expected to increase the amount of time spent at the Supermarket vegetable and fruit section. So, take the time to indulge yourself when choosing the greens that will be boosting your iron and protein intake.

Delight yourself with the sweetness of the ripe seasonal fruits and the citrus scented perfumes.

Remember: Your body is your temple. Treat it with respect. Ensure that you fuel it the best way that you possibly can.

The Newbie Veggie Must Have Tools:

Food processor or blender
Rice cooker
An oven!
Baking tray and baking pots
Frying pan
A cooking pot
Mixing bowls
A wok for our veggie stir-fries

Your Newbie Menus

The key to success for our nutritional veggie diet is variety.

The newbie starter diet includes vegetables, whole grain products, legumes, fruits, lots and lots of leafy greens, seeds and seasonal fruits.

Cold APETIZERS & Warm STARTERS

Homemade Hummus	14
Guacamole	16
Mediterranean Bruschetta's	18
Spicy Indian Mushroom Bruschetta's	20
Stuffed Aubergines	22
TTB Skewers	24
Garlic Bread	26

SOUPS & STEWS

Pea soup	30
Leek & Potato soup	32
Asparagus cream soup	34
Pumpkin soup	36
Corn soup	38
Vegetable stew	40
Courgette soup	42

SALADS

Hummus salad	46
Mushroom salad	47
Heaven salad	48
Artichoke tomato salad	49

Rice/ Quinoa Salad 50
Spinach Salad 51

MAIN MEALS

Mushroom risotto 54
Black bean lasagne 56
Ratatouille 58
Yakisoba noodles 60
Cauliflower curry 62
Enchiladas 64
Gnocchi with broccoli 66

DESSERTS

Soy Rice pudding 70
Chocolate & Mango/ banana Pudding 72
Baked caramelized apples 74
Drunken pears 76
Caramelized bananas 78
Crème Brulee 80
Chocolate almond crème tart 82

BREAKFASTS

Pancakes 86
Vegan omelette 88
French toast 90
Onion bagel with hummus 92
Sunrise with Quinoa 94

SMOOTHIES

Almond milk 98
Chocolate and almond smoothie 99
Banana and berry smoothie (using soy milk or water) 100

Cold
APETIZERS
& Warm
STARTERS

Homemade Hummus

Guacamole

Mediterranean Bruschetta's

Spicy Indian Mushroom
Bruschetta's

Stuffed Aubergines

TTB Skewers

Garlic Bread

Homemade Humus

You are going to learn in very simple and straightforward steps how to make your own tasty homemade hummus. It is fast and completely inexpensive. And you can use it as a starter, in sandwich spreads or as a base for sophisticated canapés at a dinner party. How great is that?

Ingredients for 2 people:

1 can of chickpeas (250 g)

1 lemon

1-2 garlic cloves

1-teaspoon cumin

1 teaspoon of paprika (or cayenne pepper)

A pinch of salt

1 spoonful of olive oil

1 spoonful of water (yes water!)

Chopped parsley

How do you make all these strange ingredients into hummus?

1 simple step:

Pour the can of chickpeas into a food processor, the rest of the ingredients except for the parsley. Blend well and...

MAGIC! Your homemade hummus is ready to eat! To add a bit of colour and Vitamin C now it's the time to bring in that finely chopped parsley you left behind.

Enjoy together with your favourite side- bread. Pitta works wonderfully or veggie sticks instead of bread for a lighter alternative. The choice is yours!

Guacamole

Ándale, *ándale* the perfect companion in your social gatherings.

This guacamole is one of those fantastic recipes that will help you make new friends. Fresh, super easy appetizer that won't last long!

Ingredients for 4 people:

3 ripe avocados - peeled, pitted, and mashed

1 lime

1 teaspoon of salt

½ onion (chopped)

A handful of parsley

2 small tomatoes (chopped)

1-2 garlic cloves (crushed)

1 teaspoon of paprika

Let's get dirty now, shall we?

In a medium bowl, mash together the avocados, lime juice, and salt. Add the onion and tomatoes (previously chopped) and garlic. Stir in Paprika. Add some nachos in for that Latino style appetizer and off you go!

Serve it with Tortilla chips, pita bread, or your favourite vegetable sticks. You can twist it a little by adding a few drops of tabasco for an extra quick with smoky flavour.

Mediterranean Bruschetta's

Who says that Vegans cannot have fun? Here is a bruschetta that will make you a true rock star!

Ingredients for 4 people:

8 slices of bread

2 large tomatoes (sliced)

½ red onion chopped (also called sweet onion-because it is sweet... so they say!)

2 tablespoons of olive oil

A handful of oregano (fresh if possible)

A handful of fresh basil

A handful of fresh parsley

200 g block of tofu (cut in fine slices)

Ready? 3 steps (ONLY):

1. Preheat the oven to 160 degrees C

2. In a bowl add the tomatoes, onion, olive oil, chopped oregano, chopped basil and chopped parsley.

3. Place bread on a baking sheet with the tomato mixture and some slices of tofu on top. All goes into the oven for 10 minutes.

Tick tack, tick tack... Don't make our tanned Mediterranean bruschetta's wait!

Spicy Indian Mushroom Bruschetta's

Indulge your senses with the flavours of this spicy Bruschetta brought to your table from New Delhi.

Ingredients for 4 people:

8 slices of bread

2 large tomatoes

2 small red chillies

2 teaspoons of chopped fresh ginger

1 small red onion

1 teaspoon of salt

1 teaspoon of cumin (ground or seeds)

1 teaspoon of Garam Masala

Bunch of coriander

1 small red pepper

2 garlic cloves

1 tablespoon of olive oil

2 cups of mushrooms (around 200 grams)

For Newbies

Too many ingredients to handle? Nonsense! You are a pro by now. So let's get busy!

Preheat the oven – 160 degrees C

Mix all the ingredients in a large bowl. If you feel like a real pro you can try to mix them with your own hands. Just make sure they are clean!

Place bread on a baking sheet with the mixture on top and into the oven for 10 minutes.

Aren't they mouth melting?

Stuffed Aubergine

Late in the evening, tired from work and the only thing you can think of is to have a nice shower and eat something warm?

You are about to enjoy a very special night in.

Ingredients for 1-2 persons:

1 lemon

1 garlic clove (sliced)

1 -2 aubergines (cut in half lengthwise)

1 medium size white onion

1 small red onion (chopped)

A bunch of fresh parsley

2 teaspoons of olive oil (for each aubergine half)

Ground black pepper

A small can of chickpeas (200 g)

A small can of plum tomatoes chopped (250 g)

1 small package of vegan mincemeat (you will find it in the Vegetarian section)

You like to keep things simple, right? Ok, so here you go:

To prepare the aubergine (previously cut in half lengthwise): preheat the oven 160 degrees C. score cut sides with a crosshatch pattern. Place the aubergine halves, cut sides down, on a baking tray coated with oil. Bake for 10 minutes while you prepare the filling.

To prepare the filling: combine the lemon, garlic, onion, tomatoes, chickpeas, parsley and mincemeat in a bowl and stir. Warm them up in a frying pan. Set aside.

Remove the aubergines from the oven; carefully scoop out the pulp, leaving a 0,5 cm. Season with black pepper and salt.

Fill up the aubergines with the mixture you have in the frying pan and leave it in the oven until the veggie mixture browns

Time to enjoy this lovely meal. Pair with a beer or a glass of rich red wine for extra pampering time.

TTB Skewers

The Tomato Tofu and Basil skewer recipe is so simple, quick and nutritive that you will thank me later. It is also the "unexpected guest" lifesaver!

Ingredients for 4/6 people:

Cherry Tomatoes (these are the tiny bright red tomatoes you find in the grocery stores, but any tomato really works if you don't have cherry ones, just ensure you cut them in wedges- be creative

A block of Tofu cut in Squares (around 200 g)

Bunch of basil

Olive oil

Salt

1 lemon

Ground black pepper

12 Skewers. Ready to drive? GPS on, here are the directions:

Take one skewer and add 1 cherry tomato, a basil leaf and one of those tofu squares you just cut. Repeat the process.

In a little bowl we are going to create our own sauce, yes that is right! Our own sauce! Mix the olive oil, lemon juice, salt and pepper, stir and serve.

Now spend time doing things that really matter like entertaining your guests and spreading some love!

Garlic bread

Scared of vampires? Then you have a problem because this garlic bread won't scare them off. You are warned however, garlic bread is also perfect for the yummy soups you will find in this book.

Ingredients:

1 nice French baguette

2 garlic cloves (cut in halves- remove the centre to avoid bad breath the next day)

2 spoons of olive oil

Chopped chives

A few drops of lemon juice

Now this is when the fun begins:

Pre-heat the oven 160 degrees C.

Warm the olive oil slightly in the microwave and add the chopped cloves in. We are making garlic olive oil here!

Let the oil cool down a little (to speed it up you can put the oil in the fridge for 5 minutes).

Take a little spoon and start slathering the oil all across that tasty French baguette. Be generous, go for it!

Place the bread in the oven to warm it up for 10 minutes. Your own garlic bread is now ready to be enjoyed on its own or with your favourite veggie soup.

SOUPS & STEWS

Pea soup

Leek & Potato soup

Asparagus cream soup

Pumpkin soup

Corn soup

Vegetable stew

Courgette soup

For Newbies

Making delicious soups has never been so quick and easy. I guarantee you will immediately become a fan of them. They are not only inexpensive soups but also simple and really good for you! Perfect for dinner gatherings or to warm up in cosy winter days.

You my friend are about to discover a secret you will pass onto new generations!

Pea Soup

Green colour is no longer scary and it does not mean you have to compromise on taste. This soup is packed with proteins, antioxidants, taste and every model's beauty secret.

You have come a long way now, so why not give it a try?

Ingredients for 2-4 people:

1 bag of frozen peas (250g)

1 large red onion (chopped)

1 lemon

Bunch of fresh mint

2- 3 tablespoons of olive oil

Black pepper and salt to season

500 ml water

Directions:

In a medium/large pot, add the oil and the red onion. Cook on medium heat until tender.

Add the bag of frozen peas; mix with the onions for 2-4 minutes.

Add the water, cover and bring to boiling point.

Take the pot out of the heat and blend with a food processor until smooth and add salt and pepper to taste.

Garnish with fresh mint leaves and a few drops of lemon juice.

I don't want to say it again but ... again... I TOLD YOU SO!

Serving suggestion:

And the best part is that this soup will leave you feeling filled up for a long time. You can pair it with a slice of garlic bread.

Leek & Potato Soup

A classic that has travelled all around the world here now made easier than ever before. It is low fat, creamy, healthy and it will make you feel like a newbie who knows his way around in the kitchen. Because, guess what, you do!

Ingredients for 2-4 people:

300 g potatoes (peeled and cut in cubes)

250 g leeks (chopped)

1 large red onion (chopped)

1 lemon

2-3 tablespoons of olive oil

Black pepper and salt to season

1l water

Directions:

In a medium/large pot, add the oil and the chopped red onion. Cook on medium heat until tender.

Now, add the potatoes and the leeks and cook until soft.

Add the water, cover and bring to boiling point.

Take the pot out of the heat and blend with a food processor until smooth and add salt and pepper to taste.

Because simple is simply better.

Asparagus cream soup

This soup is one of the must haves of every newbie veggie. It is delicious, healthy, low calorie, and packed with all the goodness found on earth.

Ingredients for 2 people:

250 g asparagus cut in cubes (white or green – change the colour and taste of your soup as desired, you are the painter of your masterpiece here. Just be aware green asparagus will give you a bitter taste soup)

1 large red onion (chopped)

1 lemon

2- 3 tablespoons of olive oil

Black pepper and salt to season

500 ml water

Directions:

In a medium/large pot, add the oil and the red onion. Cook on medium heat until tender.

Add the asparagus and cook until tender.

Add the water, cover and bring to boiling point.

Take the pot out of the heat and blend with a food processor until smooth and add salt and pepper to taste.

Next time try it with broccoli instead of asparagus for a change. Remember, the secret of a successful nutritious veggie diet lies in variety and creativity.

Serving suggestion:

Pair it with Garlic bread or toasted pitta.

Pumpkin / butternut soup

Pumpkin is one of those vegetables that is a symbol in autumn. It makes us think of the cold winter days that are about to come. And yet, as it is available all year around it makes for a great compliment in veggie diets.

It is loaded with antioxidants, vitamin A, C, K and E, fibre, iron and many minerals. You cannot have enough of it.

Ingredients for 2-4 people:

250 g pumpkin or pear butternut (cut in cubes)

1 large red onion (chopped)

1 lemon

2 -3 tablespoons of olive oil

Black pepper and salt to season

500 ml water

Directions:

In a medium/large pot, add the oil and the red onion. Cook on medium heat until tender.

Add the pumpkin and cook until tender.

Add the water, cover and bring to boiling point.

Take the pot out of the heat and blend with a food processor until smooth and add salt and pepper to taste.

Serving suggestion:

Serve it hot with croutons in winter and cold in summer days with a few lemon drops.

Corn soup

Excellent source of fibre and a perfect companion in spring and summer days. It will help you keep your blood pressure and cholesterol under control. And, despite its extremely low-calorie content it will leave you full for a long time. This recipe is a winner in every single aspect.

Ingredients for 2 people:

1 medium can of corn (250 g)

1 large red onion (chopped)

1 lemon

2 - 3 tablespoons of olive oil

Black pepper and salt to season

500 ml water

Parsley leaves

Directions:

In a medium/large pot, add the oil and the red onion. Cook on medium heat until tender.

Add the corn and cook until tender.

Add the water, cover and bring to boiling point.

Take the pot out of the heat and blend with a food processor until smooth and add salt and pepper to taste.

Vegetable stew

Warning: This stew is completely addictive.

It is a staple in the veggie world and can be prepared all year around and adapted to be prepared with seasonal vegetables.

Easy, tasty and keeps very well in the fridge or freezer for long periods.

Ingredients for 2 people:

2 medium potatoes (cut in squares)

2 carrots (chopped)

2 leeks (chopped)

1 pepper (chopped)

1 celery (chopped)

2 garlic cloves (chopped)

1 large red onion (chopped)

1 little can of kidney beans (or 100 g or rice previously washed as an alternative to kidney beans)

1 Lemon

2 -3 tablespoons of olive oil

Black pepper and salt to season

500 ml water

Coriander leaves

Directions:

In a medium/large pot, add the oil and the red onion. Cook on medium heat until tender.

Add the potatoes, carrots, leeks, pepper, celery, and garlic in and cook until tender. If you are replacing the kidney beans for rice, then you can add the rice at this point.

Add the water, cover and bring to boiling point.

Add the kidney beans cook for a minute and retire the soup from the heat.

Garnish with a few lemon drops and fresh coriander. Salt and pepper to taste.

Enjoy!

Courgette soup

This is a bonus family recipe that has been passed on to me and, after becoming vegan I felt my courgette soup was meant to be shared with like-minded newbies looking for some excitement in their cuisine and lives.

Ingredients for 2 people:

3 medium courgettes (chopped)

3 small potatoes (chopped)

1 large red onion (chopped)

1 lemon

2 - 3 tablespoons of olive oil

Black pepper and salt to season

500 ml water

Fresh chives

For Newbies

Directions:

In a medium/large pot, add the oil and the red onion. Cook on medium heat until tender.

Add the courgettes and cook until tender.

Add the water, cover and bring to boiling point.

Take the pot out of the heat and blend with a food processor until smooth and add salt and pepper to taste.

Serve with a few drops of lemon zest and garnish with chives!

SALADS

Hummus salad
Mushroom salad
Beans Salad
Heaven salad
Artichoke Tomato salad
Rice/ Quinoa Salad
Spinach Salad

Salads are kids play. Mamma told us not to play with our food when we were little. Well sorry to disobey but... My dear **newbie** veggie, **DO NOT GROW UP, IT IS A TRAP!**

Salads were created to bring out the best side of us, to be creative, to experiment. So lets ensure that we obey this law, shall we?

The preparation is so simple that it does not require any explanation. Just feel free to express yourself and throw in all the ingredients I am going to present you in the next pages. Of course do not just throw in the tomatoes and onions, please cut them (sliced, or in wedges for example) and simply add the olive oil, salt and pepper to taste!

Do not forget, it is all about having fun.

Serving Suggestion:

Pair with nice and warm nutty bread or our amazing garlic bread (recipe - Appetizers and starters)

Hummus salad

Ingredients for 2 people:

½ Lemon

1 bag of ready cut and washed lettuce (200g)

2 medium ripe tomatoes

1 small white onion

Fresh coriander leaves

Alfalfa broths

Soya broths (optional)

Homemade hummus (see recipe – Appetizers and starters)

A handful of Pumpkin dry seeds

Olive oil

Salt and pepper

Mushroom salad

Ingredients for 2 people:

½ Lemon

1 bag of ready cut and washed lettuce (200 g)

2 medium ripe tomatoes

Red horseradish

Fresh coriander leaves

200g mushrooms sliced

100g smoked tofu cut in cubes

A handful of sunflower seeds

Black olives

Olive oil

Salt and pepper

Heaven salad

Ingredients for 2 people:

1 bag of ready cut and washed mix salad

2 medium ripe tomatoes

1 red apple

1 green apple

A handful of crushed walnuts

A handful of cranberries

1 red onion

Fresh Basel leaves

100g smoked tofu cut in cubes

Walnut or olive oil

Balsamic vinegar

Salt and pepper to taste

Artichoke Tomato salad

Ingredients for 2 people:

5 large tomatoes

1 can or fresh marinated quartered artichoke hearts (drained)

1 can of sliced olives (drained)

A handful of parsley

A cup of dry penne pasta

2 garlic cloves sliced

Balsamic vinegar

Salt and pepper to taste

Boil 100 of dry penne pasta with salt and water until tender and set aside.

Mix all the ingredients and throw the pasta in and ...

Bon Appetit!

Rice/ Quinoa Salad

Ingredients for 2 people:

100 g (about ½ cup) of long grain rice or quinoa

1 stick of celery

1 carrot

1 green pepper

1 red onion

A handful of dried cranberries

A handful of almond flakes

A tablespoon of chia seeds (optional)

Smoked tofu cut into cubes (200 g)

Balsamic vinegar

Sesame/ olive oil

Fresh parsley

Salt and pepper to taste

Prepare the rice with water and salt or in a rice cooker. Mix with the rest of the ingredients in a big salad bowl and serve immediately. Enjoy the different textures.

Spinach salad

Ingredients for 2 people:

1 Lemon (juice)

1 bag of ready cut and washed lettuce

1 small bag of fresh baby spinach

1 red apple washed

1 orange

1 small onion

A handful of pecan nuts

A handful of raisins

Olive oil

Salt and pepper to taste

MAIN MEALS

Mushroom risotto
Black bean lasagne
Ratatouille
Yakisoba noodles
Cauliflower curry
Enchiladas
Gnocchi with broccoli

For Newbies

Food is one of the life greatest pleasures and yet some people cannot enjoy a full meal on its own without feeling guilty about it. **THINK** about this for just one second:

Food is meant to be enjoyed because it helps nourish your body so that you can make the most of your day.

So please, my dear newbie veggie, ensure that you help yourself. Avoid skipping meals.

Do not allow one single day to pass without indulging your six senses with the rich variety of food available to you.

Realise, that we should be very grateful for the food we have in our plates.

And a last plea my dear friend, do not settle for less than a proper meal every day. It is your birth right.

My message for you right here is a message of **GRATITUDE**.

Mushroom risotto

Italy is one of my favourites countries. Mediterranean cuisine inspires me a great deal. And warm, delicious, and filling, risotto is an Italian recipe with many mouth-watering variations. The recipe features wild mushrooms and fresh herbs. Serve it as a vegan dinner recipe or in smaller portions for a side dish.

Ingredients for 4 people:

1 lemon

1 white onion (chopped)

2 garlic cloves (crushed)

250 g mixed mushrooms (sliced): wild mushrooms and champignons (your creative choice here)

200 g Arborio rice

7 tablespoons olive oil (2 of them will be used for the sauce)

A handful of fresh Thyme

A handful of Oregano

500 ml water

Salt and pepper to taste

Directions:

Heat the oil in a large saucepan over medium heat. Add onion, garlic, and mushrooms. Cook, stirring often, until their water has evaporated.

Add rice and cook, stirring, for a few minutes until the rice gets a nice tan colour

Gradually add the water, stirring each time, as the rice absorbs the water.

Risotto is done when rice is tender (in aprox 25 mins)

Mix in a small bowl two spoons of olive oil and Thyme and Oregano and pour over the risotto.

Season with salt and pepper. Serve immediately.

Serving suggestion:

Decorate it with some fresh herbs and lemon zest.

Black bean lasagne

You will not get enough of this recipe. It is the perfect companion to a romantic dinner date. And this lasagne is really easy to make. It's got my *Double D rating*: Delicate and Delicious!

Ingredients for 4 people:

1 large can of kidney beans

1 can of plum tomatoes (chopped)

2 red onions (chopped)

2 garlic cloves (chopped)

1 fresh green pepper (chopped)

1 tablespoon of chilli powder

1 tablespoon of tomato puree

1 teaspoon of cumin

A handful of fresh oregano (or dry oregano)

A block of hard tofu of around 200 g (cut in cubes)

1 small cup of soymilk (200 ml)

10 lasagne sheets (follow the instructions to cook-normally just bring them to boil in salted water)

Directions:

Preheat the oven 150 degrees C.

In large bowl mix the drained beans, tomatoes, onions, garlic, pepper, chilli powder, and cumin and mix well. Set aside.

Blend with a food processor soymilk and the tofu until it becomes a paste.

Spread 1 cup of the tomato and bean mixture in the bottom of baking dish. Top with lasagne sheets and the soy cream. Repeat the process until mixtures are finished. The topcoat should be of cream soy.

Bake for 40 minutes.

Serving suggestion:

Bake until brown and serve with one of the delicious salads described previously or with a (green salad on its own). Garnish with fresh herbs and pair with a good glass of rich red wine!

Ratatouille

No, it isn't only a movie's title. It is an everlasting classic, which does not go off fashion. The amazing aspect of this dish is that you can serve it hot and cold as a main and as a starter. Not to mention all the many health benefits. The choice is wide and yours, always!

Ingredients for 2 people:

1 large tomato can peeled or chopped (500 g)

1 large white onion (chopped)

1 large red onion (chopped)

1 red pepper (chopped)

1 yellow pepper (chopped)

1 aubergine (chopped)

2 garlic cloves (chopped)

1 tablespoon of tomato puree

4 tablespoons of olive oil

A handful of fresh thyme

A handful of fresh basil leaves

Salt and pepper to taste

Directions:

Heat the oil in a frying pan over medium heat and add the onions. Cook for 2-3 minutes

Add the peppers, aubergine, cloves and tomato paste and tomato can to the pan except for the fresh herbs and cook until tender.

On low heat, cover and cook for 15 minutes, stirring occasionally.

Serving suggestion:

Serve warm either on its own or with a nice veggie stake/sausage. You can also pair with a nice piece of nutty bread and soak it in, or with rice or quinoa.

Yakisoba noodles

As a newbie veggie, you have got to love stir fries. They should be renamed *the new time saver*. They are super healthy easy noodles.

You can use whatever vegetables you have at hand. For this recipe I used cabbage, carrots, onion and mushroom.

Ingredients for two people:

250g egg free dry Soba noodles
1 small red cabbage (sliced)
1 small onion (chopped)
2 carrots (finely sliced)

2 fat garlic cloves (finely sliced)

200g button mushrooms (sliced)
1 tablespoon of sesame seeds
2 tablespoons vegetable oil

Sauce ingredients:

2 tablespoons soy sauce
2 tablespoons chilli sauce
2 tablespoons sesame oil

Directions:

Combine all the sauce ingredients in a little bowl, stir and set aside.

Bring a pan of water to boiling point and cook the noodles according to the instructions. Drain and rinse well in cold water to ensure the noodles stay loose and don't stick to each other.

In a wok and on medium heat add the vegetable oil until hot, then throw in the cabbage, onion, garlic and carrots and cook for two minutes.

Add a small amount of water and allow the veggies to steam a bit. Add the sesame seeds and stir-fry for a minute.

Add the noodles, mushrooms and sauce mixture. Cook for about 2 minutes until the noodles are hot again and serve immediately.

Serving suggestion:

To be enjoyed with your favourite drink. I love them with one of the superb smoothies presented in this book for lunches and with a nice glass of fresh citric white wine for a peaceful evening in.

Cauliflower & Lentil curry

This recipe is great when you have people around for lunch or dinner. It is guaranteed to receive many compliments. It is fresh and a highly recommended easy meal. Travel to spicy India in your own kitchen!

Ingredients for 2 people:

1 Lemon

1 onion (chopped)

1 fresh red chilly (or 2 if you like it extra hot)

2 garlic cloves (chopped)

A piece of fresh ginger (peeled and chopped)

2 teaspoons ground coriander

2 teaspoons ground cumin

1 teaspoon turmeric

1 small can red/green lentils

1 small cauliflower

1 small carrot (peeled and cut)

1 tin coconut milk

1 small cup of frozen green beans (or peas if at hand)

A handful of fresh coriander

2 tablespoon olive oil

Salt and pepper to taste

Directions:

Heat the oil in a large saucepan and gently cook the onion for 10 minutes, until soft.. Add the garlic, ginger, ground coriander, cumin and turmeric and cook for a minute. Stir continuously.

While the spices cook, heat on high heat a tablespoon of oil in a frying pan. Add the cauliflower and when slightly golden add the carrot and coconut milk.

Mix everything together in a large pan and cook for three minutes.

Salt and pepper to taste and add fresh herbs to garnish.

Serving suggestion:

This delicious dish goes with a big bowl of basmati rice by the side and any Indian bread.

Enchiladas

Feeling the warmth of the latino heart in your home?
Say no more. This recipe will make you the king or
queen of your party- whether a romantic evening or a
social gathering.

Ingredients for 2 people:

1 large red onion (chopped)

3 garlic cloves (minced)

1 medium sweet potato (chopped)

1 fresh green pepper (chopped)

1 can kidney beans (drained)

1 can of tomato sauce or enchilada sauce.

1 small fresh chilli

1 teaspoon ground cumin

1 lime

2 tablespoons of olive oil

4 tortilla wraps

Directions:

Preheat oven to 180 degrees C

Pre-cook the chopped sweet potato by simmering it in a small pot of water for about 5-10 minutes until just tender. Set aside

In a frying pan heat the oil and add the onion and cook until tender. Add the garlic, pepper and sweet potato and cook for another two minutes.

Add the tomato or enchilada sauce and cumin, fresh lime, chilli powder. Stir everything very well.

Scoop part of the mixture onto the bottom of a baking casserole dish and a tortilla, repeat the process and leave filling left to spread over the top.

Bake for around 30 minutes.

When the top browns you will know that the enchiladas are cooked. Then remove from oven and garnish with fresh chilly.

Serve with nachos, guacamole (recipe provided in appetizers and starters) and even spicy basmati rice (throw in some chillies while boiling the rice)

Gnocchi with broccoli

Feel like eating "healthy comfort food"? Is this even really possible at all? Everyone likes gnocchi and the sweet broccoli taste. Perfect for a quick dinner after a long busy day.

Ingredients for 2 people:

1 pack prepared egg free gnocchi (200 g)
Broccoli florets

3 tablespoons pine nuts (toasted if you like)

Tofu cut into cubes (200 g)

Soya sauce
Olive oil

Salt and ground pepper to taste

1 Lemon

Note: for a quicker version of this recipe, you can use smoked tofu instead of plain tofu and skip also the soya sauce.

Directions:

In a small bowl, soak in the tofu cubes in soya sauce and set aside (leave them to soak all the goodness there is in the soya sauce).

Cook gnocchi in the oven according to package directions. Add broccoli during last minute of cooking; cook for one minute. Drain.

Heat the oil in a medium size pan and add the gnocchi mixture and pepper for two minutes.

Add the tofu and cook together for an extra two minutes.

Sprinkle each serving with pine nuts and fresh drops of lemon zest.

DESSERTS

Soy Rice pudding
Chocolate & Mango/ banana
Pudding
Baked caramelized apples
Drunken pears
Caramelized bananas
Crème Brulee
Chocolate almond crème tart

For Newbies

The dessert menu could not be missed in this book. Because being vegan doe not mean that you have to renounce on pleasure. On the contrary, these recipes are heavenly and will give you *foodorgasms!*

I provide you here ingredients for 4 people. Let's be honest, if you are going to cook for yourself or for your loved ones it's always good to prepare a little extra for those occasions when we crave some sweetness. And the thing is …. Lets have these cravings because the recipes described in this book are all packed with goodness!

And… Remember to smile while eating them, because when you smile, the world will smile with you! Be happy in this present moment. Right here, right now.

Soy Rice pudding

It makes a great dessert and it is very easy to make. With a twist on the traditional non veggie recipe, soy milk and raisings tame rice pudding to a completely new level. Try it warm on those raining days and cold in the summer.

Ingredients for 4 people:

800 ml soymilk
180 g short grain rice

1 vanilla stick
100 g white or cane sugar

1 cinnamon stick

1 lemon skin
2 tablespoons raisins

Directions:

In a medium saucepan, stir together the soymilk, rice, cinnamon, vanilla sticks and the lemon skin.

Bring the mixture to boiling point, then cover, reduce heat to medium/low and simmer. Stir occasionally. Cook until the rice is tender (for around 25 minutes)

Add the sugar and raisins in.

Stir until it becomes creamy.

Pour in small pots and let them cool down covered for 10 minutes.

Serving suggestions:

Spread some ground cinnamon over it before serving and decorate with mint leaves.

Mango Pudding

Sounds very exotic and it is really easy to make. Why not doing it on a Sunday evening ready to eat after a long day at work the next day?

Ingredients for 4 people:

50 g tofu

3 ripe medium-sized mangoes

20 vegan digestive biscuits

Mint leaves

Directions:

Drain the tofu.

Peel two of the mangoes and remove the seed.

Put the mango and drained tofu into a blender and blend until smooth. If your mango was ripe, you shouldn't need to add any sugar, but if it's not sweet enough for your taste add some brown/cane sugar.

In a bowl, spread a layer of pudding down and top with biscuits. Continue alternating layers of biscuits and pudding until you run out of the cream. Ensure the top layer is pudding.

Cover and refrigerate for a few hours.

Serving suggestion:

To garnish cut the third mango and spread the slices on top of the pudding together with mint leaves.

Baked caramelized apples

We have heard many times the old "one apple a day keeps the doctor away". Caramelized apples aren't any less. A low fat dessert or snack that helps fight against heart disease and cancer. And their health benefits go further than this: they are packed with vitamin A, C, Potassium, Iron and Calcium. Truly decadent! What are you waiting for?

Ingredients for 4 people:

4 medium large red apples

1 Lemon

2 cups of sugar

Cinnamon powder

Directions:

Preheat the oven to 200 degrees C.

Wash and peel the tops and bottoms of each apple.

Place the apples in a baking tray, which previously has been oiled.

Sprinkle a little of the lemon zest into the well of each apple. Sprinkle with cinnamon and bake for 25 to 30 minutes or until tender.

While the apples are sill hot, sprinkle the sugar on top, place in the switched off oven and let the heat melt the sugar

Drunken pears

The drunken pear recipe is a perfect dessert for cold winter nights, an elegant dinner or even for a fancy brunch.

Despite their sophisticated name they are very easy to make. And it keeps for a few days in the fridge.

Ingredients for 4 people:

4-6 Pears (peeled, cored and cut in halves lengthwise)

3 glasses of Merlot or Shiraz (any red table wine works also for an inexpensive version)

3/4 cups of white sugar

1 lemon skin

2 teaspoons vanilla or 1 vanilla stick

2 teaspoons of cinnamon or 1 cinnamon stick

Directions:

Throw all the ingredients in a pot except for the pears and bring to boiling point. Once the wine is boiling, turn the heat down and add the pears.

Simmer the pears for 10 minutes or until they are tender and are easily poked through with a fork.

Remove pears and let them cool down. Boil wine sauce until the liquid has reduced by half. Pour sauce over pears and serve.

Caramelized bananas

This is one of those desserts that you can expect to find in the most exquisite restaurants and yet so inexpensive and simple to make. It guarantees a big hit in any relaxed dinner party.

Ingredients for 4 people:

2 tablespoons of coconut oil

2 tablespoons brown sugar

4 ripe and yet firm bananas (cut in halves lengthwise)

1 to 2 tablespoons honey rum or any liqueur you have at hand (e.g. almond liqueur, etc.)

Directions:

Set the grill to medium heat.

Mix the coconut oil and brown sugar in a bowl.

Lay the bananas on a baking tray and add the oil mixture. Toss generously to coat.

Grill the bananas, turning once, until a crispy brown coating of caramelized sugar forms on the surface, about 5 minutes per side.

Remove from the grill and, if you want it with an extra kick, drizzle the rum or liqueur on top.

Serve while still warm.

Serving suggestion:

Serve with a nice fruit sorbet in hot days and decorate with fresh mint leaves.

Crème Brulee

So you decided to go vegan now and you still love Crème Brulee... What a dilemma! Here is the solution and I promise you once you try, you will absolutely adore this recipe.

Ingredients for 4 people:

- 1 can coconut milk (250 ml)
- 2 tablespoon of corn flour
- 7 tablespoons sugar (save two for caramelizing)
- 1 teaspoon of nutritional yeast
- 1 stick vanilla or vanilla flavour
- 1 cinnamon stick or 1 teaspoon cinnamon powder

Directions:

Pre heat the oven 180 degrees C.

Blend all the ingredients except for the vanilla and cinnamon sticks until the mixture is soft and there aren't chunks in the cream.

Pour the mixture in a saucepan and heat.

Add the cinnamon and the vanilla.

Stir the mixture until it thickens slightly and then pour in single pots. (remove the cinnamon sticks)

Bake for 25 minutes and retire.

Let it cool down in the fridge.

To serve add some sugar on top and warm it up in the oven until the sugar melts.

Chocolate almond Crème tart

Impress your beloved ones with this glamorous sweet vegan treat.

Ingredients for 4 people:

- 1 tablet of good quality dark chocolate (250 g)
- 1 can of coconut milk
- 2 tablespoons almond liquor
- 3 tablespoons of flour
- A handful of almond flakes

Directions:

Preheat oven 150 degrees C.

Break up the chocolate bar and place it in a bowl.

In a saucepan on low heat, warm the coconut milk, sugar and almond liqueur until the mixture boils. Remove from the heat and pour the mix over the chocolate.

Wisk energetically until the clumps have disappeared (you can also use a blender or food processor to speed up the process).

Pour the crème in a baking pan or 4 small baking pots – previously oiled and bake for 20 minutes.

Chill in the fridge for a few hours.

Serving suggestion:

To serve top with cacao powder and almond flakes

BREAKFASTS

Pancakes
Vegan omelette
French toast
Onion bagel with hummus.
Quinoa with raisins, brown sugar,
and a drizzle of non-dairy milk.

For Newbies

Nutritionists can talk forever about the importance of starting the day with a complete breakfast. Media bombards us with many different coffee tastes and cereal brands for all ages that instead of making things simple only confuse us.

Let's be honest, the last thing we want to do in the morning is to think about what to eat. Most of us wake up sleepy, rush onto our daily routine and forget about breakfasts or grab something on the go or at work. And it is no biggie. After all, our bodies are still functioning. We breathe and we are alive, right?

Well you could not be more wrong. You have gotten hold of this book because you are in the process of changing and becoming a better version of yourself. And that means changes even to your morning routine. From now on, you are going to take care of yourself since the moment you are reborn every morning. And to keep things simple, I am going to present you with a list of good, energy boosting and easy to make recipes to help you with the right set of ingredients.

From now on be prepared to notice how your reactions improve, how your memory also improves, how your metabolism improves. In summary, be prepared for an improved version of a new yourself!

Pancakes

Homemade pancakes can be a great source of vitamins and carbohydrates you need to start your perfect new day.

Ingredients for 2 people:

1 cup of flour (200 g)

1-tablespoon sugar (I use organic cane sugar)

2 tablespoons baking powder

A pinch of salt

200 ml soymilk

2 tablespoons vegetable oil

Directions:

Mix the flour, sugar, baking powder, salt and soymilk until smooth in a bowl

Warm up a pan and add the oil.

Once the pan is hot, spoon one pancake worth of the mixture into the pan and wait until the edge are brown (Note that, once the edges acquire a golden colour, it will be very easy to turn the pancake over).

Then turn the pancake around, cook for a minute and retire!

Serving suggestion:

Breakkie is ready. Combine it with Jam, syrup or fresh fruits.

Vegan omelette

When I became vegan I could not stand the thought of refusing to eat omelette. Then I discovered the vegan version of the omelette- not only better and healthier than the egg omelette but also richer and very filling.

A vegan omelette can be topped, can be twisted and can be eaten as a part of a breakfast or on its own with salad or rice. Just let the creative side of you flow.

Ingredients for 2 people:

1 block of tofu (200 g)

100 ml soymilk

1-tablespoon potato starch

A pinch of onion powder

A pinch of turmeric

A pinch of salt

A pinch of paprika

Directions:

Blend together all ingredients until smooth.

Oil a pan and heat it.

Pour the creamy tofu mixture into the centre of the pan and spread with a spoon (at this point you can also add some toppings such as spinach or mushrooms for a twisted version).

Reduce the heat to low and let it cook for five minutes.

Turn over and leave it for an extra minute and ready to serve!

French toast

This is a classic breakfast recipe. Delicious, simple and anyone can make them. Once you try you will wonder why it took you so long to discover them.

Ingredients for 2 people:

200 ml soymilk

2 tablespoons flour

1 tablespoon nutritional yeast flakes

1 tablespoon sugar

1 tablespoon vanilla

A pinch of salt

A pinch nutmeg

6 slices whole wheat bread

Directions:

Pre heat the oven to 160 degrees C.

Mix the milk, flour, yeast, sugar, and vanilla, salt and nutmeg in a bowl.

Dip the bread slices into the mixture and put them in the baking tray- previously oiled.

Cook until golden, turn sides around once and let it cook again until golden (aprox 10 minutes each side)

Enjoy with your favourite smoothie, coffee or veggie hot chocolate!

Onion bagel with hummus

In search for the perfect onion bagel? It is all about having fun with your new diet choice.

Ingredients for 2 people:

2 egg free onion bagels

Homemade hummus (see recipe above- Appetizers and Starters)

Half a cucumber (sliced)

1 ripe tomato (sliced)

1 small red onion (sliced)

A handful of fresh baby spinach leaves

A handful of fresh basil leaves

Salt and ground pepper to taste

Directions:

Cut the bagels in half (you can also toast them slightly if you would like them warm).

Spread a generous amount of hummus on both halves.

Place the cucumber in one side and the tomato, red onion and spinach on the other.

Springe with salt pepper and basil leaves and serve!

Wonderful Sunday breakfast in bed.

Sunrise with Quinoa

Quinoa is our veggie superstar breakfast player. With more nutrients than any other grain and more protein and fibre than rice, quinoa positions itself in the must have grains of the newbie sporty veggie.

Ingredients for 2 people:

2 cups white quinoa

Pinch of salt

100 g of brown sugar

1 Tablespoon ground cinnamon

A handful of chopped walnuts

A handful of almond sprinkles

A handful of raisins, or dried cranberries

A pinch of salt.

Directions:

In a medium saucepan bring 4 cups of water to boiling point.

Add the quinoa with a pinch of salt once it boils, reduce the heat and cook it until soft. You can use your rice cooker as an alternative.

When quinoa is ready, add the sugar and the cinnamon and retire.

Sprinkle with walnuts, almond and raisins over the top.

Serving suggestion:

Fresh fruit to accompany if desired.

SMOOTHIES

Almond milk
Chocolate and almond smoothie
Banana and berry smoothie (using
soymilk for a milkshake or water)

For Newbies

Looking for an easy treat for a vegan indulgence?
That is what smoothies are here for! And not only that,
smoothies are the perfect drink to satisfy the need for
vitamins and fibre of the newbie vegan.

You can use fresh fruits, or frozen and still enjoy their
healthy benefits. You can drink them at home or on your
daily commute to work. And hydrate yourself.

It is important to remember that vegan smoothies are
not here to supplement your meals but to complement
them.

Here I present you with three basic recipes, the basis
of any vegan smoothie for you to play with, try, test
and create one that really works for you. And still truly
decadent when enjoyed on their own.

Almond milk

You can make a variety of plant based milks by following this simple recipe. Let it be Almonds, macadamias, hazelnuts, coconuts, pumpkin seeds, quinoa, oats... the list goes on and on, so does your imagination!

Ingredients for 4 people:
500 g almonds

2 litres water

A tablespoon of ground cinnamon

250 g sugar

Blend everything together and filter it with a sieve.

Your homemade almond milk is ready to be enjoyed very very chilled.

Rich and tasty and so good for you.

Chocolate and almond smoothie

Ingredients for 2 people:

1 ripe banana

500 ml almond milk

1 tablespoon of a good dark Cocoa Powder

A tablespoon of hard tofu

Ice cubes

Blend all the ingredients together until smooth and serve.

Banana and berry smoothie

Ingredients for 2 people:

1 ripe banana

Frozen berries or fresh berries when on season

Ice cubes

500 ml pineapple juice

A tablespoon of hard tofu

Blend all the ingredients together until smooth and serve.

For milkshake version of this smoothie you can use soymilk instead of pineapple juice.

My dear newbie veggie,

I truly hope you have enjoyed this book, which has been written with my heart and handled to you for a purpose. The purpose of love and self-appreciation. With the purpose of gratitude, fulfilment as a human being and kindness.

Being and staying a healthy and complete vegan is not that difficult. Society makes it difficult.

We are surrounded by people- call them friends, loved ones or family members- who associate vegan with lack and limitation when in fact it is quite the opposite.

Vegans take this "lack" as an opportunity to create. As a way to freely express and reinvent themselves by re-thinking how to fuel and nurture not only their own bodies but also mind and spirit.   Our bodies are a mere avatar of a bigger "self".

Love, self appreciation, gratitude, kindness and creativity and self-expression are the keys to peace and happiness in the world.

Becoming vegan, a big step.

Thank you for your help towards a better world.

With Love,

Be Kind to yourself

11377046R00065

Printed in Great Britain
by Amazon.co.uk, Ltd.,
Marston Gate.